The Ultimate Dog Diabetes Handbook for Beginners

... Managing Canine Diabetes, Understanding and Caring for Diabetic Dogs

HELEN MARSHALL

Copyright 2023

COPYRIGHT PAGE

Do not use any part of this book should in any form - electronic, mechanical or physical without an express written permission from the author.

In case of any reference to any content in this book, you should make adequate reference.

DEDICATION

I specially dedicate this book to you. Yes, you for taking out time and money to acquire knowledge.

Table of Contents

The Ultimate Dog Diabetes Handbook for Beginners 1

... Managing Canine Diabetes, Understanding and Caring for Diabetic Dogs 1

COPYRIGHT PAGE 2

Table of Contents 3

Chapter 1: Introduction to Diabetes 13

Introduction 13

The Different Types of Diabetes 13

Type 1 Diabetes 13

Type 2 Diabetes 14

Causes and Risk Factors 14

Genetic Predisposition 14

Obesity and Lifestyle 14

Age as a Factor 15

Gender Differences 15

Other Medical Conditions 15

Environmental Factors 15

Conclusion 16

Chapter 2: How Glucose Metabolism Works
.... 17

Introduction 17

Decoding the Symptoms 17

Excessive Thirst and Urination 17

Increased Hunger 18

Weight Loss 18

Lethargy and Weakness 18

Cloudy Eyes 18

Slow Healing 19

The Importance of Early Detection 19

Avoiding Diabetic Ketoacidosis (DKA)
.... 19

Improved Quality of Life 20

When to Consult a Veterinarian 20

Conclusion 20

Chapter 3: Types, Causes, and Risk Factors
.... 22

Introduction 22

The Diagnostic Process 22

    Clinical Examination 22

    Blood Tests 23

    Urinalysis..23

    Fructosamine Test.............................23

Differentiating Diabetes from Other Health Issues 24

    Cushing's Disease 24

    Kidney Disease 24

    Urinary Tract Infections 24

    Pancreatitis..25

Conclusion...25

Chapter 4: Recognizing Diabetes Symptoms 27

Introduction 27

Insulin Therapy: A Cornerstone of Treatment 27

    Understanding Insulin........................27

    Types of Insulin 28

    Insulin Administration 28

Dietary Adjustments for Diabetic Dogs 28

    The Role of Diet 28

    Carbohydrate Control 29

    Balanced Nutrition 29

Monitoring and Adjusting Treatment 29

    Blood Glucose Monitoring 29

    Adjusting Insulin Dosages 30

Consistent Care: A Key to Success 30

    Routine and Structure 30

    Regular Veterinary Check-ups 30

Conclusion 30

Chapter 5: Diagnosis and Medical Tests ... 32

Introduction 32

The Role of Diet in Diabetes Management 32

    Blood Sugar Regulation 32

    Weight Management 33

    Nutritional Balance 33

Choosing the Right Type of Dog Food 33

    Commercial Diabetic Formulas 33

    Home-Cooked Diets 33

    High-Quality Ingredients 34

Creating Balanced and Nutritious Meals 34

    Carbohydrate Management 34

    Protein Content 34

    Healthy Fats 35

Meal Planning and Portion Control ... 35

    Establish a Feeding Schedule 35

    Portion Sizes 35

    Monitoring and Adjusting 35

Conclusion 36

Chapter 6: Managing Type 1 Diabetes 37

Introduction 37

Establishing a Feeding Schedule 37

    Consistency Matters 37

    Multiple Small Meals 37

    Aligning with Insulin Administration 38

Calculating Portion Sizes 38

    Individualized Approach 38

- Consult Your Veterinarian..................38
- Monitoring and Adjusting..................38

Incorporating Treats Thoughtfully 39
- The Role of Treats 39
- Choose Low-Glycemic Treats 39
- Treats as Part of the Diet 39

Monitoring and Adapting.....................39
- Regular Blood Sugar Monitoring 39
- Communication with Your Veterinarian 40

Conclusion...40

Chapter 7: Managing Type 2 Diabetes 42

Introduction...42

The Importance of Exercise 42
- Blood Sugar Regulation.....................42
- Weight Management..........................42
- Cardiovascular Health 43

Suitable Exercises for Diabetic Dogs..43
- Low-Impact Activities 43
- Regular Moderate Exercise................43

    Avoiding Overexertion 43

Guidelines for Incorporating Exercise 44

    Consult Your Veterinarian 44

    Timing and Insulin 44

    Monitoring Blood Sugar Levels 44

Managing Blood Sugar During Exercise 44

    Hypoglycemia Risk 44

    Snacks and Quick Carbs 45

Conclusion 45

Chapter 8: Meal Planning and Nutrition 47

Introduction 47

The Significance of Blood Sugar Monitoring 47

    Individualized Treatment 47

    Early Detection of Issues 47

    Data-Driven Decision Making 48

At-Home Blood Glucose Monitoring .. 48

    Blood Glucose Meters 48

    Establishing a Routine 48

Communicate with Your Veterinarian 48

Interpreting Blood Sugar Readings....49

Target Ranges 49

Hypoglycemia and Hyperglycemia ...49

Identifying Trends 49

Challenges and Considerations...........49

Factors Affecting Readings 49

Addressing Blood Sugar Variability..50

Seek Professional Guidance 50

Conclusion...50

Chapter 9: Physical Activity and Exercise 52

Introduction..52

Preparedness for Diabetic Emergencies 52

Hypoglycemia: Low Blood Sugar 52

Diabetic Ketoacidosis (DKA)............52

The Importance of Quick Action.......53

Recognizing and Addressing Complications......................................53

Hypoglycemia Management..............53

Diabetic Ketoacidosis 53

Preventing Complications..................53

Creating a Supportive Home Environment 54

Emotional Well-Being 54

Reducing Stress 54

Social Interaction 54

Monitoring Changes and Celebrating Progress 54

Observing Changes 54

Celebrating Achievements 55

Communication with Your Vet 55

Conclusion 55

Chapter 10: Preventing Complications 57

Introduction 57

Step 1: Understanding Diabetes 57

Step 2: Early Detection and Diagnosis 58

Step 3: Treatment Options 58

Step 4: Crafting a Diabetic-Friendly Diet..58

Step 5: Meal Planning and Portion Control 58

Step 6: Exercise and Activity Guidelines 59

Step 7: Monitoring Blood Sugar Levels 59

Step 8: Managing Emergencies and Creating Supportive Environment 59

Step 9: Regular Veterinary Check-ups 59

Step 10: Celebrating Achievements and Staying Positive 60

Conclusion 60

Chapter 11: Living Well with Diabetes 61

Introduction 61

Story 1: Bella's Unbreakable Spirit 61

Story 2: Max's Journey of Transformation 62

Story 3: Luna's Heartwarming Recovery 62

Story 4: Charlie's Joyful Journey 63

Story 5: Sophie's Remarkable Resilience 63

Conclusion 64

Chapter 1: Introduction to Diabetes

Introduction

Dogs have always been cherished members of our families, offering companionship, loyalty, and unwavering love. However, like humans, dogs can also develop various health conditions, including diabetes. Understanding the intricacies of diabetes in dogs is the first step towards providing them with the care they deserve. This chapter will delve into the fundamentals of diabetes in dogs, exploring its types, causes, and risk factors.

The Different Types of Diabetes

Diabetes mellitus in dogs is primarily classified into Type 1 and Type 2.

Type 1 Diabetes

Type 1 diabetes, also known as insulin-dependent diabetes, occurs when the pancreas fails to produce sufficient insulin. Insulin is a hormone that facilitates the entry of glucose (sugar) from the bloodstream into the body's cells, where it's used as an energy source. In dogs with Type 1 diabetes, the immune system may mistakenly attack and destroy the insulin-producing cells in the pancreas, leading to a lack of insulin production.

Type 2 Diabetes

Type 2 diabetes, on the other hand, involves insulin resistance. In this scenario, the pancreas may produce insulin, but the body's cells become resistant to its effects. As a result, glucose struggles to enter the cells, causing an accumulation of sugar in the bloodstream.

Causes and Risk Factors

Understanding the underlying causes and risk factors of diabetes in dogs is crucial for prevention and early detection.

Genetic Predisposition

Certain breeds are genetically predisposed to diabetes. Species like Pomeranians, Beagles, Miniature Schnauzers, and Dachshunds have a higher risk of developing diabetes. This genetic susceptibility highlights the importance of regular check-ups for at-risk breeds.

Obesity and Lifestyle

Obesity plays a significant role in developing Type 2 diabetes in dogs. Just like humans, dogs that lead sedentary lives and consume calorie-dense diets are more prone to obesity and subsequent diabetes. Maintaining a healthy weight through balanced nutrition and regular exercise is a critical preventive measure.

Age as a Factor

As dogs age, their risk of developing diabetes increases. Middle-aged to senior dogs are more susceptible to the disease. This emphasizes the need for regular veterinary visits and health assessments as your furry friend ages.

Gender Differences

Female dogs are believed to have a slightly higher predisposition to diabetes than males. However, diabetes can affect both genders and vigilance in monitoring for symptoms is essential for all dogs.

Other Medical Conditions

Certain medical conditions, such as Cushing's disease and chronic pancreatitis, can increase the likelihood of diabetes in dogs. These conditions can impair the normal function of the pancreas and disrupt insulin production.

Environmental Factors

Environmental factors, including diet and exercise, play a significant role in a dog's overall health and susceptibility to diabetes.

Feeding your dog a balanced diet and regular exercise can significantly reduce the risk of diabetes development.

Conclusion

Understanding the types, causes, and risk factors of diabetes in dogs is the foundation for providing optimal care and support to your furry companion. Whether it's the immune-mediated destruction of insulin-producing cells or lifestyle-related insulin resistance, recognizing the factors contributing to diabetes empowers you as a responsible dog owner. As we move forward in this handbook, we will delve deeper into the signs and symptoms of diabetes, diagnostic procedures, and the array of treatment options available to ensure a happy and healthy life for your diabetic dog.

Chapter 2: How Glucose Metabolism Works

Introduction

Dogs are known for masking discomfort, making detecting health issues challenging for pet owners early on. In the case of diabetes, timely recognition of symptoms is crucial for effective management and to prevent complications. In this chapter, we will explore the common signs and symptoms of diabetes in dogs, delve into the importance of early detection, and discuss when to consult a veterinarian.

Decoding the Symptoms

Excessive Thirst and Urination

One of the hallmark signs of diabetes in dogs is polydipsia (excessive thirst) and polyuria (excessive urination). You may notice your dog drinking water excessively and needing to urinate more frequently. This occurs because elevated blood sugar levels lead to the kidneys working overtime to eliminate the excess sugar, causing increased urine production and triggering thirst.

Increased Hunger

Despite eating regularly, diabetic dogs might experience increased hunger. This paradox happens because the body's cells cannot effectively use glucose for energy due to insufficient insulin. The body compensates by signalling a need, hoping to obtain more power from food.

Weight Loss

Diabetic dogs may undergo unexplained weight loss, even if their appetite has increased. This occurs because the body starts breaking down fat and muscle tissue for energy without sufficient glucose utilization. If your dog is losing weight despite eating well, it's a red flag to consider.

Lethargy and Weakness

High blood sugar levels can lead to a lack of energy and overall lethargy in dogs. You might notice a decrease in your dog's activity level, a reluctance to engage in physical activities, and a general sense of weakness. This is due to the body's inability to use glucose effectively for energy production.

Cloudy Eyes

Diabetic dogs are prone to developing cataracts, leading to cloudy or opaque eyes.

Cataracts form due to elevated blood sugar levels affecting the eye's lens. If you observe any changes in your dog's eyes, particularly a sudden cloudiness, consult a veterinarian promptly.

Slow Healing

Diabetes can compromise the body's ability to heal efficiently. Minor cuts, wounds, or infections might take longer to heal in diabetic dogs due to impaired immune function and reduced circulation. Monitoring the healing process closely can provide valuable insights into your dog's health.

The Importance of Early Detection

Recognizing the early signs of diabetes can improve your dog's quality of life. Early detection allows for prompt intervention and management, preventing the disease from progressing and causing more severe complications.

Avoiding Diabetic Ketoacidosis (DKA)

Without timely intervention, diabetes can lead to diabetic ketoacidosis (DKA). DKA occurs when the body breaks down fat for energy, releasing ketones into the bloodstream. Elevated ketone levels can lead to a life-threatening condition characterized by vomiting, dehydration, and coma. Early detection and proper management significantly reduce the risk of DKA.

Improved Quality of Life

Managing diabetes early prevents complications and ensures that your dog can enjoy a good quality of life. By stabilizing blood sugar levels and addressing symptoms, you can help your dog maintain energy, engage in activities, and avoid the discomfort associated with uncontrolled diabetes.

When to Consult a Veterinarian

If you observe any of the symptoms mentioned earlier, it's essential to consult a veterinarian without delay. Professional expertise is crucial for accurately diagnosing and formulating an appropriate treatment plan. Early intervention can prevent the disease from progressing and improve the chances of successful management.

Additionally, regular veterinary check-ups are essential, especially for senior dogs and those at a higher risk of diabetes due to breed predisposition. Routine blood tests can detect subtle changes in blood sugar levels before overt symptoms develop, enabling proactive management.

Conclusion

Recognizing the symptoms of diabetes in dogs requires a keen eye and a deep understanding of your furry friend's behaviour. From excessive thirst and urination to unexplained weight loss, these signs are vital clues that something might be amiss. By heeding these signals and seeking veterinary attention promptly, you can ensure your dog receives the care needed to manage diabetes effectively. In the upcoming chapters, we will explore the diagnostic procedures used to confirm diabetes, the various treatment options available, and how to create a diabetes-friendly environment for your beloved canine companion.

Chapter 3: Types, Causes, and Risk Factors

Introduction

Accurate diagnosis is the cornerstone of effective management regarding your dog's health. In the case of diabetes, a timely and precise diagnosis lays the foundation for a tailored treatment plan that can lead to a better quality of life for your furry companion. This chapter will explore the diagnostic process for dog diabetes, the various testing methods employed, and how to differentiate diabetes from other health issues.

The Diagnostic Process

Clinical Examination

A comprehensive clinical examination is the starting point for diagnosing diabetes in dogs. Your veterinarian will consider your dog's medical history, breed predisposition, and the symptoms you've observed. This holistic approach helps rule out other potential causes of the symptoms.

Blood Tests

Blood tests play a pivotal role in diagnosing diabetes. A blood sample is analyzed to measure blood glucose levels. However, diagnosing diabetes isn't as straightforward as just measuring blood sugar. The timing of the blood draw for meals and activities is crucial. Elevated blood glucose levels, particularly after fasting or consuming food, can indicate diabetes.

Urinalysis

Urinalysis provides valuable insights into your dog's health. In diabetes, glucose is excreted in the urine due to high blood sugar levels. A urinalysis can detect the presence of glucose in the urine, which is a strong indicator of diabetes. Additionally, urinalysis helps assess kidney function and identify potential urinary tract infections.

Fructosamine Test

The fructosamine test measures the average blood glucose levels over the past two to three weeks. This test helps provide a broader perspective on blood sugar control and can complement other diagnostic methods.

Differentiating Diabetes from Other Health Issues

Cushing's Disease

Cushing's disease, or hyperadrenocorticism, shares some symptoms with diabetes, such as increased thirst and urination. Distinguishing between the two conditions is crucial, as their management approaches differ significantly. Cushing's disease involves an overproduction of cortisol, a stress hormone. Blood tests and additional diagnostics can help differentiate between diabetes and Cushing's disease.

Kidney Disease

Kidney disease can also lead to increased thirst and urination. A thorough examination and blood work can help determine if the underlying cause is diabetes or kidney-related issues. In some cases, dogs with diabetes might develop kidney problems as a complication, highlighting the importance of accurate diagnosis.

Urinary Tract Infections

Urinary tract infections can cause similar symptoms to diabetes, such as increased urination. A urinalysis can help determine if the symptoms are due to a disease or diabetes. Treating your dog with a urinary tract infection might alleviate the symptoms, but further investigation is essential to rule out or confirm diabetes.

Pancreatitis

Pancreatitis is inflammation of the pancreas and can impact insulin production. Dogs with pancreatitis might display symptoms resembling diabetes, including decreased appetite and lethargy. Distinguishing between the two conditions requires a combination of clinical evaluation, blood tests, and potentially imaging studies.

Conclusion

The diagnostic journey for diabetes in dogs involves a blend of clinical observation, blood tests, urinalysis, and potentially more specialized tests. Accurate diagnosis is essential to differentiate diabetes from other health issues with similar symptoms. Remember that a diagnosis of diabetes isn't a cause for panic; instead, it's an opportunity to implement effective management strategies. The insights gained from diagnosis lay the groundwork for tailoring treatment plans that can improve your dog's well-being and enable them to lead a fulfilling life despite the challenges of diabetes. As we proceed through this handbook, we will explore the diverse treatment options available for diabetic dogs, empowering you with the knowledge to make informed decisions for your beloved pet's health.

Chapter 4: Recognizing Diabetes Symptoms

Introduction

Managing diabetes in dogs requires a multifaceted approach encompassing medical care, nutrition, and lifestyle adjustments. Effective treatment aims to regulate blood sugar levels and enhance your dog's overall quality of life. This chapter will delve into the various treatment options available for dogs with diabetes, focusing on insulin therapy, dietary adjustments, and the importance of consistent care.

Insulin Therapy: A Cornerstone of Treatment

Understanding Insulin

Insulin therapy is a fundamental aspect of managing diabetes in dogs. Insulin, a hormone produced by the pancreas, plays a crucial role in facilitating the entry of glucose into cells. For dogs with diabetes, insulin injections are often required to replace the inadequate or absent natural insulin production.

Types of Insulin

Several types of insulin are available for dogs, each with its characteristics and duration of action. Short-acting insulin, such as regular insulin, acts quickly but requires more frequent administration. Intermediate-acting insulin, like NPH insulin, has a longer duration of action and is typically administered twice daily. Long-acting insulin, such as insulin glargine, offers steady coverage and may be given once a day.

Insulin Administration

Administering insulin to your dog requires precision and care. Your veterinarian will guide you on the correct dosage, injection technique, and frequency. Insulin injections are usually given subcutaneously, which means under the skin. Proper strategy and a consistent schedule are essential to maintain stable blood sugar levels.

Dietary Adjustments for Diabetic Dogs

The Role of Diet

Diet plays a pivotal role in diabetes management. A balanced and carefully planned diet can help regulate blood sugar levels, prevent weight gain, and contribute to your dog's overall well-being. Consult your veterinarian to determine the most suitable diet for your diabetic dog.

Carbohydrate Control

Controlling the intake of carbohydrates is crucial for managing blood sugar levels. Diabetic dogs benefit from diets that have a controlled and consistent carbohydrate content. High-fibre diets can slow glucose absorption, preventing rapid spikes in blood sugar after meals.

Balanced Nutrition

Ensuring your dog receives all the necessary nutrients is essential for their health. Diabetic dogs require a diet that maintains a healthy weight while meeting their nutritional needs. Combining lean proteins, healthy fats, and complex carbohydrates can provide energy without causing rapid blood sugar fluctuations.

Monitoring and Adjusting Treatment

Blood Glucose Monitoring

Regularly monitoring your dog's blood sugar levels is crucial to diabetes management. Blood glucose meters designed for dogs allow you to measure blood sugar levels at home. Your veterinarian will guide you on how often to test and how to interpret the results.

Adjusting Insulin Dosages

Monitoring blood sugar levels provides insights into whether the current insulin dosage is adequate. Based on these readings and your veterinarian's guidance, adjustments to the insulin dosage may be necessary. Close communication with your veterinarian ensures your dog's treatment plan is tailored to their specific needs.

Consistent Care: A Key to Success

Routine and Structure

Dogs thrive on routine, and diabetic dogs are no exception. Establishing a consistent way for meals, insulin injections, exercise, and monitoring helps stabilize blood sugar levels. Predictability in their daily life contributes to better diabetes management.

Regular Veterinary Check-ups

Regular veterinary visits are essential for assessing your dog's progress, making necessary adjustments to the treatment plan, and addressing any concerns. These check-ups allow your veterinarian to monitor your dog's overall health and ensure that diabetes management remains effective.

Conclusion

Managing diabetes in dogs requires medical intervention, dietary adjustments, and consistent care. Insulin therapy is often at the heart of treatment, helping regulate blood sugar levels and providing the energy needed for your dog's daily activities. Dietary choices play a significant role in maintaining stable blood sugar levels and overall health. By closely monitoring blood sugar levels and making necessary adjustments, you can ensure that your dog's treatment plan remains adequate. Consistent care, routine, and regular veterinary check-ups contribute to your dog's well-being and offer them the chance to lead a fulfilling life despite the challenges of diabetes. As we move forward, we will explore the intricacies of crafting a diabetic-friendly diet, planning meals, and incorporating exercise to create a well-rounded care plan for your furry companion.

Chapter 5: Diagnosis and Medical Tests

Introduction

A well-crafted diet is a cornerstone of managing diabetes in dogs. The food your dog consumes directly influences their blood sugar levels, energy levels, and overall health. This chapter will explore the importance of a diabetic-friendly diet, how to choose the right dog food and strategies for creating balanced and nutritious meals that support your dog's well-being.

The Role of Diet in Diabetes Management

Blood Sugar Regulation

A diabetic-friendly diet plays a crucial role in regulating blood sugar levels. Foods with a controlled and consistent carbohydrate content help prevent rapid spikes in blood sugar after meals. This stability is essential for managing diabetes and reducing the risk of complications.

Weight Management

Maintaining a healthy weight is vital for dogs with diabetes. Obesity exacerbates insulin resistance and makes blood sugar control more challenging. A carefully planned diet that provides essential nutrients without excess calories supports weight management.

Nutritional Balance

A balanced diet ensures your dog receives all the nutrients necessary for optimal health. Protein, healthy fats, vitamins, and minerals contribute to your dog's overall well-being and play a role in maintaining energy levels and supporting immune function.

Choosing the Right Type of Dog Food

Commercial Diabetic Formulas

Several commercial dog food brands offer specialized diabetic formulas designed to support blood sugar control. These formulas often have controlled carbohydrate content and a balanced nutrient profile. Consult your veterinarian to determine if a commercial diabetic recipe suits your dog.

Home-Cooked Diets

Some dog owners prefer to prepare home-cooked meals for their diabetic dogs. While this approach allows for greater control over ingredients, it requires careful planning to ensure the diet is nutritionally complete and supports blood sugar regulation. Consult a veterinary nutritionist to create a balanced home-cooked diet.

High-Quality Ingredients

Regardless of the type of diet you choose, prioritize high-quality ingredients. Look for dog food that lists meat as the primary ingredient, avoiding fillers and excessive additives. Whole grains, vegetables, and healthy fats contribute to a well-rounded diet.

Creating Balanced and Nutritious Meals

Carbohydrate Management

For diabetic dogs, managing carbohydrate intake is paramount. Complex carbohydrates with a low glycemic index are preferable, as they have a slower impact on blood sugar levels. Vegetables like sweet potatoes, peas, and carrots can be included in moderate amounts.

Protein Content

Protein is essential for maintaining muscle mass, supporting immune function, and promoting overall health. High-quality animal-based proteins, such as chicken, turkey, and lean beef, are excellent choices.

Protein also has a minimal impact on blood sugar levels.

Healthy Fats

Incorporate healthy fats into your dog's diet to provide energy and support skin and coat health. Fats from sources like fish, flaxseed, and coconut oil are beneficial. However, be mindful of portion sizes to avoid excess calorie intake.

Meal Planning and Portion Control

Establish a Feeding Schedule

Creating a consistent feeding schedule helps regulate blood sugar levels. Divide your dog's daily food intake into several small daily meals. This approach prevents dramatic spikes and drops in blood sugar and provides a steady energy source.

Portion Sizes

Your veterinarian can guide you on the appropriate portion sizes based on your dog's size, activity level, and nutritional requirements.

Monitoring and Adjusting

Monitor your dog's response to the diet by regularly measuring blood sugar levels and observing their overall well-being. Adjust portion sizes and meal frequency to maintain stable blood sugar levels and optimal body condition.

Conclusion

Crafting a diabetic-friendly diet for your dog is a proactive step toward effective diabetes management. By choosing the right type of dog food, focusing on balanced and nutritious ingredients, and paying attention to portion sizes, you can support your dog's blood sugar control, weight management, and overall health. Please consult your veterinarian to tailor a diet plan that addresses your dog's specific requirements and fits their lifestyle. In the upcoming chapters, we will explore the intricacies of meal planning, portion control, and incorporating treats while managing blood sugar levels. Your commitment to providing a nutritious and well-balanced diet will contribute significantly to your diabetic dog's health and well-being.

Chapter 6: Managing Type 1 Diabetes

Introduction

Crafting a diabetes-friendly diet is not just about choosing the right foods; it's also about planning meals and controlling portion sizes to ensure stable blood sugar levels. In this chapter, we will delve into the intricacies of meal planning for diabetic dogs, establishing a feeding schedule, calculating portion sizes based on factors like size and activity level, and incorporating treats to align with blood sugar management.

Establishing a Feeding Schedule

Consistency Matters

A regular feeding schedule helps regulate blood sugar levels by providing a predictable source of glucose and insulin needs.

Multiple Small Meals

Dividing your dog's daily food intake into several small meals can help prevent dramatic fluctuations in blood sugar. Instead of two or three large meals, opt for four to six smaller meals throughout the day.

Aligning with Insulin Administration

If your dog is receiving insulin injections, coordinate their meals with the timing of the injections. This synchronization helps ensure that glucose entering the bloodstream from food aligns with the presence of insulin, promoting better blood sugar control.

Calculating Portion Sizes

Individualized Approach

Calculating portion sizes for a diabetic dog requires an individualized approach. Factors such as age, weight, activity level, and insulin sensitivity all play a role in determining the appropriate amount of food.

Consult Your Veterinarian

Your veterinarian is your best resource for determining the correct portion sizes for your dog. They can provide guidance based on your dog's specific needs and can make adjustments as your dog's condition changes over time.

Monitoring and Adjusting

Regularly monitoring your dog's blood sugar levels helps you assess whether portion sizes are appropriate. If blood sugar levels are consistently too high or too low, it might indicate that adjustments to portion sizes are necessary.

Incorporating Treats Thoughtfully

The Role of Treats

Treats are an excellent way to bond with your dog and offer positive reinforcement. However, in the context of diabetes management, treating requires careful consideration to prevent blood sugar spikes.

Choose Low-Glycemic Treats

Opt for treats with a low glycemic index, meaning they have a slower impact on blood sugar levels. Vegetables like carrots, green beans, and cucumbers can make excellent low-calorie, low-carbohydrate treats.

Treats as Part of the Diet

Rather than offering treats separately from meals, consider including them in your dog's daily calorie and carbohydrate intake. This approach helps maintain better control over their overall nutrient intake.

Monitoring and Adapting

Regular Blood Sugar Monitoring

Blood sugar monitoring remains essential as you adjust your dog's meal plan and portion sizes. The data you gather helps you make informed decisions and track the effectiveness of the dietary approach.

Communication with Your Veterinarian

Regular communication with your veterinarian is crucial when changing your dog's meal plan. Your vet can guide, analyze blood sugar trends, and ensure that your dog's diet supports their diabetes management.

Conclusion

Meal planning and portion control are vital components of managing diabetes in dogs. Establishing a consistent feeding schedule, calculating portion sizes, and thoughtfully incorporating treats are all strategies that contribute to stable blood sugar levels and overall well-being. Remember that each dog's needs are unique, and adjustments may be necessary as you observe your dog's response to dietary changes. Open communication with your veterinarian is critical to tailoring a meal plan that aligns with your dog's health goals. In the subsequent chapters, we will explore the significance of exercise and activity, how to monitor blood sugar levels, and strategies for managing emergencies that might arise in diabetes care. Your commitment to crafting a well-rounded care plan reflects your dedication to providing the best possible life for your beloved diabetic dog.

Chapter 7: Managing Type 2 Diabetes

Introduction
Physical activity is a powerful tool in the management of diabetes in dogs. Exercise supports weight management and plays a role in regulating blood sugar levels and promoting overall health. This chapter will explore the importance of exercise for diabetic dogs, suitable practices, and guidelines for incorporating physical activity into their routine while ensuring optimal blood sugar control.

The Importance of Exercise
Blood Sugar Regulation
Regular exercise can help improve insulin sensitivity, allowing the body to use glucose more effectively. Physical activity encourages the muscles to absorb glucose from the bloodstream, lowering blood sugar levels.

Weight Management
Maintaining a healthy weight is vital for diabetic dogs, as obesity can exacerbate

insulin resistance and complicate blood sugar control. Exercise supports weight management by promoting calorie expenditure and lean muscle mass.

Cardiovascular Health

Exercise improves cardiovascular health by improving circulation, heart function, and overall fitness. This is particularly important for dogs with diabetes, as they may be at a higher risk of cardiovascular complications.

Suitable Exercises for Diabetic Dogs

Low-Impact Activities

Low-impact exercises are gentle on joints and are well-suited for dogs with diabetes. Walking, swimming, and soft play sessions fall into this category.

Regular Moderate Exercise

Consistency is critical when it comes to exercise. Engaging in regular moderate activity helps regulate blood sugar levels over time. Aim for daily sessions of about 20 to 30 minutes, gradually increasing the duration as your dog's fitness improves.

Avoiding Overexertion

While exercise is beneficial, overexertion can have adverse effects. Avoid intense activities that might cause exhaustion or excessive stress on joints.

Guidelines for Incorporating Exercise

Consult Your Veterinarian

Before implementing an exercise routine, consult your veterinarian to ensure that your dog's overall health and diabetes management plan allows for physical activity. Your vet can guide suitable exercises and potential limitations.

Timing and Insulin

Consider the timing of exercise for insulin administration and feeding. Exercising shortly after a meal might help prevent blood sugar spikes. However, monitor your dog's blood sugar levels closely, as exercise can also cause glucose levels to drop.

Monitoring Blood Sugar Levels

Blood sugar monitoring is critical when introducing or modifying an exercise routine. Regular monitoring helps you understand how exercise affects your dog's blood sugar levels and allows for timely adjustments to insulin dosages and meals.

Managing Blood Sugar During Exercise

Hypoglycemia Risk

Exercise can increase the risk of hypoglycemia (low blood sugar) in diabetic dogs. Vigilance is essential during and after physical activity to detect any signs of hypoglycemia, such as weakness, confusion, or shakiness.

Snacks and Quick Carbs

A small, easily digestible snack during exercise can help prevent hypoglycemia. Quick sources of carbohydrates, such as glucose gel or honey, can rapidly raise blood sugar levels in case of a hypoglycemic episode.

Conclusion

Incorporating regular exercise into your diabetic dog's routine is a powerful tool for managing their condition and improving their overall well-being. By engaging in suitable practices, adhering to guidelines, and closely monitoring blood sugar levels, you can help regulate blood sugar, support weight management, and enhance cardiovascular health. Remember that exercise should be gradual, consistent, and tailored to your dog's needs and limitations. As we progress through this handbook, we will explore the nuances of monitoring blood sugar levels during exercise, managing potential emergencies, and creating a diabetes-friendly home environment that supports your dog's health and happiness. Your commitment to providing well-rounded care demonstrates your dedication to ensuring the best possible life for your beloved diabetic dog.

Chapter 8: Meal Planning and Nutrition

Introduction

Effective diabetes management relies on maintaining stable blood sugar levels. Regular blood glucose monitoring provides crucial insights into your dog's response to treatment, diet, and exercise. This chapter will delve into the importance of monitoring blood sugar levels for diabetic dogs, the tools and techniques for at-home monitoring, and how to interpret the readings to make informed decisions.

The Significance of Blood Sugar Monitoring

Individualized Treatment

Every dog's response to diabetes management is unique. Blood sugar monitoring allows you to tailor treatment to your dog's needs, adjusting insulin dosages, meal plans, and exercise routines.

Early Detection of Issues

Regular monitoring helps you detect trends and patterns in your dog's blood sugar levels. This lets you catch potential issues early and take proactive steps to prevent complications or hypoglycemic episodes.

Data-Driven Decision Making

Blood sugar readings provide valuable data that guides your decisions. By analyzing these readings and understanding how factors like meals and exercise impact blood sugar, you can make informed choices that support your dog's well-being.

At-Home Blood Glucose Monitoring

Blood Glucose Meters

Blood glucose meters designed for dogs are available for at-home monitoring. These meters measure blood sugar levels from a small blood sample obtained through a quick, painless prick of the dog's ear or paw.

Establishing a Routine

Consistency is essential when monitoring blood sugar levels. Establish a routine for testing, aiming for the exact times each day to gather reliable data.

Communicate with Your Veterinarian

Share your blood sugar readings with your veterinarian during check-ups or whenever adjustments to the treatment plan are considered. Your vet can help you interpret the data and make informed recommendations.

Interpreting Blood Sugar Readings
Target Ranges

Blood sugar target ranges vary depending on factors such as the dog's age, overall health, and the type of diabetes. Consult your veterinarian to determine the appropriate target range for your dog.

Hypoglycemia and Hyperglycemia

Understanding the signs of both hypoglycemia (low blood sugar) and hyperglycemia (high blood sugar) is essential. Hypoglycemia symptoms include weakness, confusion, and trembling, while hyperglycemia symptoms might involve increased thirst and urination, lethargy, and poor appetite.

Identifying Trends

Regular blood sugar monitoring lets you identify trends in your dog's readings. Consistently high or low blood sugar levels may indicate the need for adjustments to the treatment plan.

Challenges and Considerations
Factors Affecting Readings

Keep in mind that various factors can affect blood sugar readings. Stress, illness, changes in routine, and other medical conditions can influence results. Try to control as many variables as possible to obtain accurate data.

Addressing Blood Sugar Variability

It's common for blood sugar levels to vary from day to day. Rather than focusing on individual readings, pay attention to trends and overall patterns over time.

Seek Professional Guidance

Consult your veterinarian if you encounter challenges or have concerns about blood sugar readings. They can help you troubleshoot issues and ensure your monitoring technique is accurate.

Conclusion

Monitoring blood sugar levels is a fundamental aspect of managing diabetes in dogs. By establishing a routine, using blood glucose meters, and interpreting readings, you gain valuable insights into your dog's health and can make informed decisions regarding their treatment plan. Remember that blood sugar readings provide a snapshot of your dog's condition at a particular moment; analyzing trends over time is critical to understanding how various factors impact blood sugar levels. Regular communication with your veterinarian ensures that your monitoring efforts align with your dog's needs and contribute to their well-being. As we progress through this handbook, we will explore managing emergencies related to blood sugar, creating a supportive home environment, and fostering emotional and psychological well-being for you and your diabetic dog. Your commitment to diligent monitoring reflects your dedication to providing the best care for your beloved furry companion.

Chapter 9: Physical Activity and Exercise

Introduction

Living with a diabetic dog requires preparedness for emergencies and creating an environment supporting their well-being. In this chapter, we will explore the importance of being equipped to handle diabetic emergencies, understanding the signs of complications like hypoglycemia and diabetic ketoacidosis, and creating a supportive home environment that fosters emotional and psychological health.

Preparedness for Diabetic Emergencies

Hypoglycemia: Low Blood Sugar

Hypoglycemia, or low blood sugar, can occur suddenly and lead to severe complications if not addressed promptly. Common signs include weakness, confusion, trembling, and even seizures.

Diabetic Ketoacidosis (DKA)

DKA is a life-threatening condition that can arise when blood sugar levels are consistently too high. Symptoms include vomiting, rapid breathing, lethargy, and a distinctive fruity breath odour. DKA requires immediate veterinary attention.

The Importance of Quick Action

In both hypoglycemia and DKA cases, quick action is essential. Having a plan and knowing the steps to take can save your dog's life. Keep emergency contact information for your veterinarian or an emergency clinic readily available.

Recognizing and Addressing Complications

Hypoglycemia Management

If you suspect hypoglycemia, immediately offer a small, easily digestible carbohydrate source. This could be glucose gel, honey, or even a treat high in simple sugars. Monitor your dog's response and seek veterinary care if symptoms persist or worsen.

Diabetic Ketoacidosis

DKA requires immediate veterinary intervention. Do not attempt to treat DKA at home. Contact your veterinarian or an emergency clinic when you recognize the symptoms.

Preventing Complications

Consistent blood sugar monitoring, accurate insulin administration, and adhering to a well-balanced diet and exercise routine significantly reduce the risk of complications.

Creating a Supportive Home Environment

Emotional Well-Being

Caring for a diabetic dog involves more than just physical health. Emotional well-being is essential, too. Maintain routines, offer affection, and engage in activities your dog enjoys to foster a positive emotional state.

Reducing Stress

Stress can impact blood sugar levels, so minimizing sources of stress is essential. Keep routines consistent, provide a quiet and comfortable space, and monitor your dog's reactions to situations.

Social Interaction

Interacting with other dogs and people can improve your dog's psychological health. Socialization helps prevent feelings of isolation and supports a positive emotional state.

Monitoring Changes and Celebrating Progress

Observing Changes

Stay attuned to changes in your dog's behaviour, appetite, energy levels, or overall demeanour. Early detection of changes allows for timely intervention and management adjustments.

Celebrating Achievements

Managing diabetes is an ongoing journey, and celebrating even small achievements is essential. Recognize improvements in blood sugar control, weight management, or overall well-being as victories.

Communication with Your Vet

Regular communication with your veterinarian is critical to managing your dog's condition and creating a supportive environment. Share observations, seek guidance, and maintain open lines of communication.

Conclusion

Managing diabetes in dogs involves the physical aspects of treatment and the ability to address potential emergencies and create a supportive environment that nurtures their emotional and psychological health. Being prepared for emergencies like hypoglycemia and recognizing the symptoms of complications like DKA can significantly affect your dog's outcome. Additionally, creating a supportive home environment that emphasizes routines, minimizes stress, and prioritizes emotional well-being contributes to your dog's overall quality of life. By closely monitoring changes, celebrating progress, and maintaining open communication with your veterinarian, you can ensure that your dog's journey with diabetes is as positive and fulfilling as possible. In the final chapter of this handbook, we will bring together all the knowledge you've gained to outline a comprehensive roadmap for successfully managing diabetes in your beloved dog, ensuring a future filled with love, care, and optimal health.

Chapter 10: Preventing Complications

Introduction

As you journeyed through the previous chapters of this handbook, you've gained a deep understanding of managing diabetes in your dog effectively. In this final chapter, we will bring together all the knowledge you've acquired to create a comprehensive roadmap that outlines the key steps, strategies, and principles for successfully navigating the challenges of diabetes management. Following this roadmap can provide your beloved dog with the best possible care and support their optimal health and well-being.

Step 1: Understanding Diabetes

Begin by educating yourself about diabetes in dogs. Please familiarize yourself with the basics of the condition, including its causes, symptoms, and potential complications. This foundational knowledge will serve as the cornerstone of your diabetes management journey.

Step 2: Early Detection and Diagnosis

Recognize the early signs of diabetes and the importance of prompt diagnosis. Regular veterinary check-ups, blood tests, and urinalysis are crucial for identifying diabetes early and initiating treatment to prevent complications.

Step 3: Treatment Options

Understand the various treatment options, including insulin therapy, dietary adjustments, and exercise. Work closely with your veterinarian to create a tailored treatment plan for your dog's needs.

Step 4: Crafting a Diabetic-Friendly Diet

Design a well-balanced diet that supports blood sugar regulation, weight management, and overall health. Choose high-quality ingredients, control carbohydrate intake, and monitor portion sizes to meet your dog's nutritional needs.

Step 5: Meal Planning and Portion Control

Establish a consistent feeding schedule, calculate portion sizes, and incorporate treats thoughtfully. Meal planning and portion control contribute to stable blood sugar levels and support your dog's diabetes management plan.

Step 6: Exercise and Activity Guidelines

Incorporate regular, low-impact exercise into your dog's routine to improve blood sugar regulation, maintain a healthy weight, and promote cardiovascular health. Consult your veterinarian to determine suitable activities and timing.

Step 7: Monitoring Blood Sugar Levels

Regularly monitor your dog's blood sugar levels using at-home blood glucose meters. Establish a routine, interpret readings, and adjust treatment, diet, and exercise based on the data you gather.

Step 8: Managing Emergencies and Creating Supportive Environment

Be prepared to handle diabetic emergencies like hypoglycemia and recognize the symptoms of complications such as diabetic ketoacidosis. Create a supportive home environment that prioritizes emotional well-being, reduces stress, and fosters a positive relationship with your dog.

Step 9: Regular Veterinary Check-ups

Schedule regular check-ups with your veterinarian to assess your dog's progress, make necessary adjustments to the treatment plan, and address any concerns. Your veterinarian's expertise is essential for long-term diabetes management.

Step 10: Celebrating Achievements and Staying Positive

Celebrate the milestones and progress your dog makes along the diabetes management journey. Stay positive, patient, and committed to providing the best care possible for your beloved canine companion.

Conclusion

Successfully managing diabetes in your dog requires a comprehensive approach that encompasses medical care, dietary adjustments, exercise, emotional well-being, and vigilant monitoring. By following this roadmap, you can navigate the challenges of diabetes with confidence, compassion, and competence. Remember that each dog's journey is unique, and adjustments may be necessary. Your commitment to providing consistent care, open communication with your veterinarian, and unwavering love reflects your dedication to your furry friend's health and happiness. As you embark on this journey, know that you have the knowledge and tools to ensure a bright and fulfilling future for your diabetic dog.

Chapter 11: Living Well with Diabetes

Introduction

In this final chapter, we are honoured to share inspiring stories of canine resilience and triumph over diabetes. These stories are a testament to the strength of the human-canine bond and the incredible capacity of dogs to adapt, thrive, and overcome challenges. As you read through these narratives, you'll witness the determination, love, and care that have transformed the lives of these dogs and their devoted owners. May these stories serve as a source of encouragement, motivation, and hope for your journey of managing diabetes with your beloved canine companion.

Story 1: Bella's Unbreakable Spirit

Bella, a lively Labrador Retriever, was diagnosed with diabetes at a young age. Sarah's owner was determined to provide Bella with the best care possible. They learned to adjust insulin dosages and crafted a balanced diet. Bella's boundless energy and indomitable spirit shone through as she embraced her new routine. With Sarah's dedication and Bella's resilience, they overcame challenges, celebrated victories, and demonstrated that a diabetes diagnosis was merely a new chapter in their adventure together.

Story 2: Max's Journey of Transformation

Max, a charismatic Golden Retriever, faced a life-altering diagnosis of diabetes in his senior years. His owner, Mark, recognized the importance of exercise and worked with their veterinarian to create a tailored fitness plan. Max's daily walks became a cherished ritual, fostering his physical and emotional well-being. Through consistent monitoring and adjustments to his diet and insulin regimen, Max not only managed his diabetes but also experienced a remarkable improvement in his overall vitality. Mark and Max's journey is a testament to the transformative power of determination and a loving partnership.

Story 3: Luna's Heartwarming Recovery

Luna, an affectionate Poodle, faced a critical moment when she developed diabetic ketoacidosis (DKA). Her owner, Emily, recognized the situation's urgency and rushed her to the veterinarian. After intensive treatment and recovery, Luna emerged more vital than ever. Emily's vigilance, quick action, and unwavering support were pivotal in Luna's remarkable turnaround. Their story illustrates the importance of understanding the signs of complications, seeking immediate veterinary care, and the resilience that can emerge from the darkest moments.

Story 4: Charlie's Joyful Journey

Charlie, a spirited Jack Russell Terrier, faced the challenges of diabetes with a heart full of joy. His owner, Lisa, embraced a holistic approach that included dietary adjustments, exercise, and emotional well-being. Charlie's zest for life was evident as he enthusiastically participated in activities, basked in affection, and thrived despite his diagnosis. Lisa's dedication to providing a supportive environment and nurturing Charlie's emotional health enriched their bond and showed that a positive attitude can make a difference in managing diabetes.

Story 5: Sophie's Remarkable Resilience

A gentle Cocker Spaniel, Sophie demonstrated remarkable resilience in the face of diabetes. Her owner, James, meticulously monitored her blood sugar levels, adjusted her diet, and collaborated closely with their veterinarian. Despite the challenges, Sophie's unwavering trust in James and his commitment to her well-being paved the way for a successful diabetes management journey. Sophie's story showcases the profound impact of a solid human-canine connection and the potential for triumph over adversity.

Conclusion

These stories of canine resilience and triumph over diabetes remind us that the journey is not defined by the challenges we face but by the love, dedication, and care we pour into our furry companions. Each story underscores the importance of understanding diabetes, seeking veterinary guidance, crafting a tailored care plan, and embracing a positive outlook. Just as these dogs have shown incredible strength and adaptability, so too can you and your beloved dog navigate the complexities of diabetes management with grace and determination. As you embark on your journey, may these stories serve as a beacon of hope and inspiration, guiding you toward a future filled with joy, health, and an unbreakable bond with your diabetic dog.

Printed in the USA
CPSIA information can be obtained
at www.ICGtesting.com
LVHW020203241024
794698LV00008B/256